REMEMBER LOVE

REMEMBER LOVE

LOVE

Words for Tender Times

CLEO WADE

HARMONY

NEW YORK

Library of Congress Cataloging-in-Publication Data

Names: Wade, Cleo, author.
Title: Remember love: words for tender times / Cleo Wade.
Description: First edition. | New York: Harmony, [2023] |Summary: "The
beloved, bestselling author of Heart Talk, hailed as "the poet of her
generation" (Time), charts a path away from exhaustion and endless crises
and toward a place of renewal and radiant love with a new, soulful collection
of original poetry and prose"—Provided by publisher.
Identifiers: LCCN 2023007362 (print) | LCCN 2023007363 (ebook) |
ISBN 9780593581360 (hardcover) | ISBN 9780593581377 (ebook)
Subjects: LCSH: Self-acceptance. | Love. | Relaxation.
Classification: LCC BF575.S37 W334 2023 (print) |
LCC BF575.S37 (ebook) | DDC 158.1—dc23/eng/20230623
LC record available at https://lccn.loc.gov/2023007362
LC ebook record available at https://lccn.loc.gov/2023007363

ISBN 978-0-5935-8136-0
Ebook ISBN 978-0-5935-8137-7
Barnes & Noble ISBN: 978-0-5937-9683 2

Printed in the United States of America

Book design by Andrea Lau
Jacket design by Kaitlin Kall

10 9 8 7 6 5 4 3 2 1

First Edition

This book is dedicated to my readers, my friends.

Us, always.

CONTENTS

Poetry was my therapy before I could afford a therapist. Every time I have wondered, "How on earth am I going to get through this?" I turned to paper and pen. It is not possible to know the answers to all of life's questions or problems. Most of them don't even have answers, they simply request that we let go, learn from, or live with what happens to us. Because of that, I have found that what we really need is comfort and good company as we make our way. We are tender beings living in a tender time. I think a lot of us are wondering, "How on earth am I going to get through this? How on earth are we going to get through this?"

It is helpful to believe that you and we will get through this. It is also helpful to know that you are not alone. I wrote this book in hopes it could offer a hand to pull you up if you feel stuck, a companion that will be by your side and walk with you no matter where you're going or what you are going through.

cleo wade

REMEMBER LOVE

PART ONE

eventually we get there

We get lost. Often. It just happens. And it's okay. The heart work we do for ourselves isn't done to avoid the tough stuff—periods of lostness, self-doubt, sadness, grief, and anxiety. We learn to love ourselves so we can handle these periods. So that our discomfort doesn't block our healing. So that lostness is not our permanent state and is instead a starting point for self-discovery.

homecoming

I said

she'll be fine

too many times
so
she left me
and when she came back

she was worn

and tired
and looking for

warm arms

to wrap around her
and even though
I didn't recognize her

at first
I held her

and we became reacquainted
I apologized and I promised

to look after her

and take care of her

cleo wade

I promised her we'd always find each other

and I let her know that she may get lost

but she won't stay lost

the love within you will always welcome you home

I know how to love myself on a regular day feeling like my regular self, but nothing really prepares you for how to feel good about yourself when you don't feel like yourself.

It is hard to love a stranger. It is extra hard when change has turned the stranger into you.

Lying awake in the night, my racing heart grabbed my inner megaphone and repeated the words "something is wrong with you" so loudly they echoed through my bones.

It was a lie that felt true, and I couldn't unhear it.

Self-love is often spoken about like a battle we either win or we lose, but it manifests more as a bird in flight. It is minute to minute. There are moments we glide through the sky, riding the wind with ease, and there are moments we must exhaust our wings to survive the elements.

On my worst days, I forgot I had wings.

I believed every negative thing I thought whether it made sense or not.

In hopes of finding a little comfort during my tough time, I ran a bath one night and put on a talk by Tara Brach, a meditation teacher and psychologist I have listened to for over a decade.

As I sat, staring at the ceiling for half an hour, kind of listening, kind of not, I heard two words that jolted me from the haze of my brain fog:

Remember Love.

It was as if she had not said a single word except these for the past

thirty minutes. *Remember Love.*

I write because I know the power of words. Words have saved me

every time I needed saving.

These two words did something to me. They saved me. I began to

ask myself if I could remember love. When life changes, can I re-

member love? When I change, can I remember love? When my

relationships change, can I remember love? When I remember

love, I remember I am resilient.

I can love myself through a hard time. I know this because I have

done it. I remember that my spirit is soft but durable. I remember

that my love belongs to me when I am at my sturdiest and my

most fragile. I remember that my life is bigger than whatever noise surrounds me. I remember that clear days have always followed my storms (even when the storms felt like hurricanes).

I remember love, and I remember my wings.

I remember I can fly.

findings

feeling lost
reminds us
we have a home

a place within

waiting & willing
to
welcome us & shelter us

a place within

where we
eternally & unconditionally
belong

a place within
where love
begins
and never
ends

cleo wade

The old Motel 6 commercials always ended with the same slogan:

We'll leave the light on for you.

Life, depression, anxiety, grief, trauma, addiction, numbing, and avoidance are all more complicated than a motel slogan. But I do believe that when we feel far from home, when we are wondering, *who am I and what the hell am I doing with my life,* there is an eternal light left on within. It may feel faint, it may feel nonexistent, you may need help finding it, but it's there. If your road has been long and you are in your darkest hour, close your eyes, put your hand on your heart, and say to yourself, I'm on my way. Hear the reply: We'll leave the light on for you.

To live is to get lost.

The shimmery, magical part of this inevitability is the reunion.

The power to embrace yourself time and time again. To sit in the safety of a room all your own, wrapped in a soft blanket of okayness, receiving your warm welcome home.

You get to come home to yourself. Know that.

**for people like me who don't know
how to relax**

I hear whispers from shadows high and low
no one seems to know where they come from
but they surround us and seem to be getting louder

get busy, they say

do something!

do nothing
and
you are nothing

I plant my feet into our earth
I place my hand on the tree that
gives life to me
I let its ancient wisdom remind me
of real power
and I speak light into these shadows

no, I say

I am not built for only doing
I am built for being
I am built for loving

I raise my fist and within it I hold

stillness and worthiness together as one
belonging to each other and belonging to me

my rest does not need a reason
my goodness does not need to be proven
my value is mine to claim

so
I will be
and I will love

and the soul within me
connected to the earth beneath me
will be the loudest voice in my head

we do not have to listen to the shadows just because we can
hear them

Some of us were able to pause during the great pause of our world. Some had to go into overdrive, creating new ways to protect and support ourselves and loved ones. Others channeled fear and anxiety into hobbies and projects.

I painted rooms dramatic colors like dark green, tried and failed to complete a weekly journaling club, I even went through a Lego phase and built the Hogwarts Castle (six thousand pieces!).

Somehow the waves of anxiety, grief, fatigue, and despair felt more manageable if I was doing something. *Anything.*

I thought all of my doing was a great plan until I sat down and tried to write. My advice for writing has always been to show up. I tried. Day after day. I would show up, but the pages were blank.

Nikki Giovanni's advice for writing is to relax.

That, I hadn't tried.

Life doesn't give us much space to relax. Each hour of the day, our phones spill everything from strangely addictive baking videos to footage of social-political uprisings into the palm of our hands.

Her advice to relax disarmed me because honestly it reminded me that relaxation was even on the table.

Being busy, exhausted, and distracted had become my norm. Being outside of myself had become my norm. I think we do this when we are scared or stressed. We leave ourselves behind because facing ourselves means facing our feelings.

If I stopped doing, I'd have to feel my fear and my worry.

When we disconnect from ourselves because we want to avoid uncomfortable emotions, we lose our ability to thoroughly tap into the light and joy that also live within us.

I needed to reconnect.

I started by trying to relax. I stepped away from the pace of the world (and the scroll of the internet) so I could find a pace that my *self* could be felt.

It was not easy or easeful but to love ourselves is to continuously reclaim ourselves. No matter what.

I don't want to be a busy body. I want to be a body.

I want to be in spaces I feel alive, not numb, even when aliveness

is hard.

We go through periods of disconnection and lostness, but we are

all worthy of returning to ourselves.

TO LOVE OURSELVES IS TO
CONTINUOUSLY RECLAIM
OURSELVES. NO MATTER WHAT.

something big

I stopped searching

for things

things I thought should
belong to me

I started sitting

in gratitude

for what surrounded me

the falling leaves
the flowers, the break in the sidewalk
the endless sky, moody and magnificent

these forces of nature
remind me I am one too

with relief, I release the small stuff

very little belongs to me
and I belong
to something big

cleo wade

I spent the weekend with a friend in Fire Island a few years ago and witnessed a beautiful ritual amongst the neighbors. On their shared dock, they gathered to watch the sunset each evening and clapped as it disappeared below the horizon.

It moved me to tears. Tears for earth's beauty. Tears of awe and appreciation for the soulful respect shown to earth's beauty.

I think we love sunsets so much because they remind us that we belong to mother nature, she doesn't belong to us. She is your mother and you are her child.

To be alive and connected to something so vast is a stunning gift.

We rarely search for ease. We may even be suspicious of something that feels easeful. The outside world often tells us that difficulties and discomfort make life more valuable and love more worthwhile. There is wisdom to be found in and on the other side of our struggles, but we can also grow, learn, and become without harshness. Can we reframe ease as a sign that something feels right instead of wrong? Can we make ease a destination for our relationships and decision making? Can ease be the goal in the midst of a challenge? Ease is the space where our flow and our peace live as one.

daisies (the happiest flower)

the world can be unforgiving and untender,
some are good at loving and some are lousy

find ease
live in it wherever you can get it

if what is in front of you is
a field of flowers

frolic, beloved

The culture and industry of busy-ness is a powerful force that can lead us far from ourselves.

Being overscheduled, overworked, and excessively online has become a way of life, but it is not sustainable.

It feels like we are at a breaking point, which makes sense.

If a car is stuck in drive, the only way it can stop to be refueled or repaired is by breaking down or crashing.

We shouldn't have to break down in order to pour into ourselves. When we recognize this, we understand the incredible value of rest and restoration.

A synonym for restoration is return.

The nature of being busy is to do, to expend only outward energy.

It is easy to lose track of yourself in this.

The nature of rest is to be.

It is a return to yourself.

some types of sadness

some
types of sadness

appear and vanish
a quick hello & goodbye

some
types of sadness

linger like a moon
cycling through its phases
in your being

full
half
a sliver
barely there
but
there

do not lose hope
for on the darkest night
the lightless moon
is also
the new moon

something is on the way

There is an artist in my hometown named Bmike, who has a large painting on the side of a wall downtown that says, "they tried to bury us, they didn't know we were seeds."

Our difficulties may derail us, we may even feel as if they are burying us; resilience is the knowingness that we are seeds. That we grow through whatever we go through. We break the soil and reach toward the light.

a small and mighty truth

going through it
is often how
we get to
the other side of it

remember this when you want to give up

cleo wade

here

as a kid in school, I hear my name during roll call, I raise
    my hand, and, loud enough to be above the noise, I say

present!

I think about that now.

present!

present, here I am.

today I am older
and
have made it through
some things

sorrow moved in for a while
and brought lots of luggage

nevertheless

present
here I am

a tornado of my worst thoughts rolled through
and left me breathless
present
here I am

there has been a lot I've seen
and heard and felt
that hurt

present
here I am

and

here you are

you have made it through some things
we have made it through some things

present
here
here we are

One definition of the word recovery is to regain possession of something stolen or lost.

We all go through periods of trying to recover time.

Could be the time we feel was wasted in a relationship or the time we wish we were nurtured better in our childhood. Many of us are wondering how to recover the time we felt was lost to life inside over the past few years.

In my family and community, we have talked a lot about personal lostness during these times.

I feel as though I have been on a journey to reclaim myself over these past years. A self in a new phase of life, a self that is trying to navigate an ever-changing world, a self that is mustering up the courage to find a sturdy path outdoors after years inside the house.

There is so much to heal from, so much we have all been through.

Somehow reading the definition of recovery made me feel more hopeful.

We are in recovery. Yes. That's it. This is a recovery period. We are going to feel a little off as we navigate new selves, goals, and perspectives on life.

We need recovery periods.

They create the space and pace for necessary healing. I find that when I am resisting the global recovery we are living in, I feel defeated. I feel like something is wrong. When I allow myself to be in recovery and am okay with feeling different and needing different tools and maps to move forward, I find a little peace even in my discomfort.

RECOVERY IS A SPIRITUAL DANCE
WITH CHANGE. IT IS ONE STEP
AT A TIME. A PUSH AND A PULL.
AN INTIMATE MOVEMENT TOWARD
A MORE TENDER RELATIONSHIP
WITH YOURSELF.

day by day

our bodies
and the life that flows through them
are seasonal

the sun stays a little longer
what's ice begins to melt

yes

there is still and chill in the air

but

do not worry

your winter
is becoming
spring

I can't think of anything comfortable about the healing process. We move slowly and feel impatient. We are tired and feel frustrated. We don't feel like ourselves.

It is really disorienting.

Our body's physical healing process is also incredibly emotional. I recently realized I held a lot of shame around the change of pace physical and mental healing requires.

We have to slow down to heal. Often, we have to pause to heal. Easier said than done. I used to get the blues every time I was home sick with a common cold.

I remember feeling sad and restless in bed after an emergency surgery to remove my appendix the week before my thirtieth birthday. I even struggled to slow down during my pregnancy and postpartum periods. I was living in London when I was pregnant with my first daughter and after a work trip to Rwanda, I came home and insisted we meet friends at Carnival in Notting Hill. I was six months pregnant and so run down I fainted on the street. Fortunately my partner caught me before I hit the pavement. I was in denial that I was physically different and therefore needed to move through the world differently.

I often feel like my journey through postpartum depression would have been less daunting if I hadn't tried to rush the healing process. If I had learned earlier how to be okay with needing slowness. Or sooner reckoned with my insecurities, which desperately linked worthiness to productivity.

ve don't see

t see everything
aren't supposed to
e
belongs
squares
ded by lovers, enemies, and passersby
rs
is the only remedy
secrecy
a hiding
ozy nest
ply cannot fit
ld

cleo wade

On the other side of these e

therapy and immense suppor

tude for what the healing pro

Changing pace in our fast-n

greatest challenges. It has also

When we slow down, we give

more life. More healing. More

we do
and w
for sor
healin
in tow
surrou
for oth
privac
it is no
it is no
it is a
that si
the wo

you never know

too many of us
are smiling on the other side of
our struggles
even more of us
are in an absolute moment
of courage
smiling
in the midst of
our struggles

a couple reasons your neighbor needs your kindness

anyway

life is a tough blessing
tough and important and sweet
filled to the brim with humor, tragedy, and calamity
anyway
it is a blessing
hold tight to the blessing part in all of this

Big beginnings and big endings change us. We do not get to stay who we were. Not for forever and often not for long. Go where you feel called to go. Do what you feel moved to do. Be with who you need to be with. Find okay-ness. Give yourself space and permission to be okay. When the sky is pouring unfamiliarity over everything, don't let it soak you to the bone. Take cover. Find shelter.

it's simple

every
time
you change
get to know yourself
again

A dedication to self-discovery is an anchor connecting us to ourselves.

We are endlessly getting to know who we are. Like every living thing, we are growing in each moment and are never the same as we were yesterday.

Are you interested in yourself?

You are worthy of your own curiosity.

When we stop being curious about our inner life, our relationship with ourselves becomes stale and distant.

We get off track. We take ourselves for granted. We assume we know ourselves so we stop noticing and paying attention to our new thoughts, dreams, and even aversions.

When we habitually travel inward, that journey brings clarity to everything we encounter.

There are times we feel like we don't belong in our own lives because an old version of ourselves chose our current job, friends, living situation, or romantic relationship. If you feel like you are adrift, you can always come back to yourself. You belong to and with yourself.

Get to know yourself as you would a friend. What do you like? Which relationships feel good? Which don't?

This spiritual investigation is a reminder that you are someone you love. You are someone who benefits from your care and concern.

Stuck-ness feels like running towards a locked door.

Can you slow down, walk, or stand still for a minute?

Catch your breath.

Question the door, the room, the journey.

Do you feel stuck because you expected the door to look different?

Is it possible to have a completely different relationship with next steps? Can you entertain every possible option, even the ones that feel "crazy"?

Do you even need to get to the other side of this door to move forward? In the room, is there someone who can help? Can you release the judgments you have about the journey that led you here?

Can stuck-ness be your obstacle and not your identity?

People (like me) who pride themselves on being "doers" often experience healing periods as moments of brokenness, and maybe they are, but what is wrong with being in pieces?

Sometimes we need to break things apart in order to understand the value of each piece so we can redesign the whole.

The energy of life is a building and a breaking down that keeps us more often in the process than in the result. I wish we could always feel whole ("doers" love to have everything feel buttoned up and perfectly in place), but I have found that there is deep love and incredible wisdom in the space between the pieces. The space where we can ask and answer soulful questions.

The truth is, we are built to break and we are built to be able to put ourselves together again, even if it's in a way that is radically different than it was before.

We rise, we fall, we change, we bloom—this is the process of healing. It is nature and it is our nature.

yours, truly

as you go on
forward, backward, sideways
up, down, nowhere, somewhere
be kind to yourself
self-kindness is the companion that will always say

there, there, my love

when you need those words

more than anything

NOT EVERY CHANGE IS A
TRANSITION. SOME ARE REBIRTHS.
AND A REBIRTH, LIKE ANY OTHER
BIRTH, HAS SOME PAIN BUT ALSO
A LOT OF MAGIC.

over & over

life is loving you

she is a mother giving
birth to you

over & over again

with every rebirth

she holds you
covering your beating heart
and breathing body
with a prayer that says,

sameness
is not your destiny,
dear one
aliveness is

When I was pregnant, a spiritual teacher I'd been seeing told me that my daughter's birth would be my rebirth.

I'd never really considered the idea of being reborn in my one lifetime.

I'd thought about rebirth in terms of reincarnation. I'd felt before that I knew someone so instantly and intimately that surely we'd spent a past life or two together. I'd scooted a giant spider in my writing room into a cup and released it outside, with the logic that if I saved it, I would avoid coming back as a spider in my next life.

But more than one life in my current incarnation? This was new.

And there was something about it that felt right. I thought about times in my life I have struggled with transition. Even the idea of transition made me think of struggling, like a tug-of-war between

my past and present selves. A lot of tension, a lot of holding on, a

lot of second-guessing.

Something about the idea of a rebirth feels so liberating. Like I

don't have to stretch myself in opposite directions. Like I could

just breathe into a new world and let it all feel different and okay.

There have been a few rebirths for me in this life. When I finally

quit my day job and became the writer I am today, I was reborn.

The first time my heart broke and I had to put it back together all

by myself, I was reborn.

I didn't have the language to call it a rebirth then, but I wish I had.

It would have helped me make sense of my sorrow and confusion as I desperately tried to hold on to outdated relationships, friendships, and ideas about myself that no longer belonged.

Many moments in life cause us to be reborn—grief, tragedy, triumph, big birthdays, milestones in our children's lives, divorce, falling in love, sobriety and the healing of addiction and abuse.

Can we allow ourselves to be reborn again and again in this life? Can we courageously sit in the discomfort of knowing that there will be times when nothing feels the same?

Maybe you are going through a rebirth right now and you feel like you are experiencing every relationship, including the one with yourself, for the first time.

As someone in the same boat, I want to let you know it is okay.

And over time it becomes more than okay, it becomes the thing you didn't know you needed, but needed the most.

Happy Birthday.

PART TWO

worthy rebellions

ENOUGH-NESS IS NOT A
MOUNTAIN. IT IS A MIRAGE OF A
MOUNTAIN. WE DO NOT NEED TO
CLIMB IT, WE NEED TO SEE
THROUGH IT.

it's an everyday thing

can I say

"I love you"

to myself
not only on the days the sun is shining
and
the gold medal is around my neck

but
on the days
life
is covered in clouds

no finish lines, no prizes

just me

still here
here, still

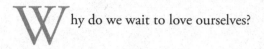

Why do we wait to love ourselves?

Can we love ourselves without feeling like we need to be right, perfect, or good? Can we love ourselves whether or not we have the right job, car, house, body fat percentage, relationship, or family life?

We don't need to earn our own love. It is our birthright. It wholly belongs to us no matter our circumstances. External validations don't lead us closer to love, we lead ourselves closer to love. It is within us. We connect to it by going inward.

Love waits within, she is like a favorite auntie, whether you haven't seen her in a day or a year, she opens her arms to you for a big hug and says, "okay, tell me everything"

I know how easily and quickly we can get disconnected from love.

When we feel sad, anxious, or depressed, it is hard to locate love beneath our symptoms.

There have been times over the past couple years when I thought, if I could just feel less tired, or if my brain fog would just dissolve, then I could feel okay with myself.

Then I could love myself.

I'd forgotten that it is in those moments, I need my own love the most. The truth is, we need our love every day, regardless of how insecure we may feel. It is our stabilizing force.

If we think we always have to be more in order to be loved, we will never be able to accept love. Not from ourselves or anyone else.

You already deserve to love and respect yourself. Befriend yourself,

love who you are today. No matter what it looks like.

what's held

you call yourself the glue

but while
you
hold it all together

who

is holding

you?

cleo wade

I often hear people say with pride that they are the glue, the person who keeps everything together in their family or friend group.

I am one of those people.

But what does that really mean?

Glue is a sticky, tacky, gunky substance. The nature of it is stuckness. When we are being the glue—doing the lion's share of the emotional and domestic labor, organizing everyone's lives, working around the needs of others without considering our own—we turn ourselves into a utility.

We are a tool for our family rather than a person in our family.

Glue is the substance that holds things together. If you are holding

things together right now, know that you, too, deserve to be held.

We all deserve to be held. And we need to be held.

Those who really love us want a chance to show up for us even if

they aren't in the habit of doing so. And if they don't know how,

they will learn—if they want to. If they don't, that's a whole other

story.

I don't think anyone who loves us wants us to feel like the glue.

They want us to feel like a part of the family.

A part of life.

YOU WILL ONLY FEEL BEHIND IF
YOU THINK THERE IS ONE TRAIL
THAT LEADS TO THE TOP OF THE
MOUNTAIN. THERE ARE MORE
WAYS TO GET TO WHERE YOU
WANT TO GO THAN YOU COULD
POSSIBLY IMAGINE. YOU MOVE
FORWARD BY FOCUSING ON YOUR
PATH.

M ary Oliver said, "things take the time they take."

There is no one way or right time. There is *your* way and *your* time.

I have friends who go through breakups quickly and decisively. They just leave when it is time to go. I have friends who take years to wade out of relationships. I have friends who can be jolted out of sadness, and friends whose inner light is on a dimmer switch slowly becoming brighter and brighter over time.

When I have moved through bouts of anxiety and most recently postpartum depression, feeling better on my own time line has been what I needed most.

When I am in the midst of sadness, trying something hard, or doing something brave, I am the kind of person who needs to tiptoe into the shallow end and slowly submerge. I don't think I have done a cannonball in my entire life. Even with risk. I have taken huge risks but have done so with thoughtful consideration for my fragilities. I have learned I can swim in amazing depths, if I can get there in my own way and at my own speed.

Things take the time they take.

Whether it is the time you need to heal, move, read a book, commit to a relationship, leave a relationship, have kids, go back to school, switch jobs.

When you respect your process, you honor your needs, you honor yourself, you honor your precious life.

in a world

I am tired of feeling strong
I want to feel nourished

I want to feel like my body is a soft, tender body
and not armor

I want to feel like my body is a soft, tender body
and not a machine

I want to stretch my arms
I want to feel the sun on my face

I want to hear a song that reminds me of myself
I do not get what I want each day

but I manage to leave the chill of the shadows
I manage to find the sun for at least a little while
&
I am grateful that

I still know how to want
something gentle and grand for myself
in a world that tells me
I have to be strong and small to survive.

I still know how to be a flower in a world
that tells me I must be made of steel to survive

soften if you can

you've been hiding
your hurt feelings
so long
who could find them?
you've been building these walls
so tall
who could climb them?

come out where we can see you, come out where we can
    feel you, we've been waiting to love you

e hide.

We hide using physical distance, burying ourselves in work, not leaving the house, ignoring texts, dropping the ball on plans with people who want to spend time with us.

We hide in plain sight. We hide by being overly helpful. We hide by being the giver not the receiver. We hide by making the joke instead of having the cry. We hide by having it all together because deep down we feel like everyone is allowed to fall apart except us.

We build walls around our softness, because we think that only our strength can survive in the world.

I hate to say it, but we aren't entirely wrong.

There are plenty of rooms and relationships that only our strength can survive in.

Our softness doesn't belong everywhere, but it does belong *somewhere*.

It belongs in your home, the home within you, the home you build with your people. It belongs in your friendships and romantic relationships.

When I am speeding around at 110 miles an hour, I try to slow down and ask myself why.

What am I hiding from? Who am I not letting in? Am I doing because I am struggling to feel lovable? Am I working to earn love because I feel I don't deserve it as I am?

We do a lot of hiding, forgetting that most hiding places are in the

dark, not in the light.

We deserve to move into the light, where love can find us.

LIKING AND LOVING OURSELVES
IS OUR GREATEST
RESPONSIBILITY. IT GIVES US THE
POWER TO WALK IN THE WORLD,
HONEST AND ALIVE,
MASQUERADING AS NO ONE, WITH
NO MOTIVE BUT TO DO GOOD, FEEL
GOOD, AND WANT FOR OTHERS
THE SAME WARMTH WE FEEL
FROM THE CANDLE WE HAVE LIT
WITHIN.

Just because something is in our capacity does not make it our responsibility.

How you feel about what you take on is important.

We have all lived through some inauthentic yeses that should have been nos. We have all impulsively said yes to something we either didn't want to do or didn't have the energy to do.

Knowing and respecting our limits is how we avoid becoming martyrs in our work, friendships, and family dynamics. It is what keeps the poison of resentment out of our bodies and our peace protected.

It is up to you to know how much is too much. That is a boundary only you can make.

You have to know when to take stuff off your list, when to put yourself at the top of your list, and also, perhaps, when to throw it out and live outside of a list.

that sounds great

let's build a life we can live in

a life with
space for soulfulness

a life that has a home
filled with people who really know
each other
where our friends become

our family
and
our family
become our friends

where the kitchen is our kitchen and
our dance floor

we laugh and we laugh
even when we cry
we laugh and we laugh

let's build a life
we can live in

surrounded by seasons
and their offerings
a magnolia in bloom

a bird that hums and hovers

the sun warming us

from the inside out

we talk about the important things

isn't this pasta delicious?
have you heard this song?
can I read you this poem?

let's build a life
we can live in

one that doesn't move too fast
because
you can't enjoy anything in a hurry

joy
is unhurried

Someone with a demanding job recently asked me how he could make his limited time with his family more meaningful. He told me each night he makes a minute-to-minute list and schedule for his workday and had been trying to do the same type of planning for his relationships. I told him the strategies for a productive workday don't usually work for creating deeper connection with those we love. Relationships live outside of our lists and org charts. We can't have an efficiency mindset when it comes to loving others. Love is slow. It is warm, tender, patient, and surprising. It requires our time and most relaxed self. The us that can just be. The us that can listen and witness. The us that is a home and can be a home to others. A sweet shelter.

IN BALANCE, WE TURN OUR LIFE
INTO A SCALE, CONSTANTLY
MOVING AND MEASURING.
IN HARMONY, WE TURN OUR LIFE
INTO A SONG. EVERY SOUND IN
THE SONG BELONGS.

I don't believe in balance.

Balance is often marketed to us as the ultimate goal for a happy life, but as a recovering perfectionist, I find that chasing balance leaves me feeling out of breath and not enough. It turns my life into a scale and takes me out of being present with the people around me. I feel tense and rigid as I relentlessly measure how much time I should spend on what.

When we treat time spent on our work or family life like something we pass or fail each day, we will almost always feel like failures.

And, believe me, I have tried.

I have lived by time slots in my calendar, obsessing over magic scheduling formulas I thought would give me the "right" amount of time for my work, my friends, my family, myself.

It was an endless pursuit.

Life doesn't fit in boxes. Life is a wild animal, or a mighty oak tree with unruly roots. We don't tame it. We find harmony with it.

Harmony is a fluid acknowledgment that everything present is a part of the whole.

It allows for movement, flexibility, and grace.

I still plan and goal-set, but I also allow for life to do what life does and look different every day. I don't think something is wrong with it or me when my expectations aren't met. I accept that I will come up short sometimes and so will everybody else. I accept that

stuff happens. Stuff that might turn my day or my life upside

down.

Choosing harmony allows for me to exist within the melody of my

life.

YOUR ROLE IS TO BE IN YOUR
LIFE, NOT CUT AND MEASURE IT.
IF WE ARE ALWAYS DOING THE
MATH, WE ARE NEVER PART OF
THE EQUATION.

A magazine asked Gloria Steinem how she defines success.

She said, "It's the moment when you feel you are doing something you care about, that you can be honest, and that you're able to live in the moment."

I often use these words to anchor me to a more purposeful perspective. They remind me that a big part of success is following what feels good. It feels good to do things we care about. It feels good to be honest, and it feels good to live in the moment. Her recipe for success could just as easily be a recipe for happiness.

At the end of the day, isn't a happy life a successful one?

When the material is at the center of my goals, I cross the finish line, and even if I am holding the first-place trophy, there is some loneliness there. But when the relational is at the center of my goals, whether I finish first or last,

I am what's held.

A friend and I were on the phone discussing the difficulties of finding okay-ness in stillness when it feels like everyone around you is relentlessly producing.

We talked about her father, a legendary musical performer who has had an enduring career. I asked how she thought he and his peers were able to make such relevant, high-quality work for so many decades. She said she thought it was because they took time away in between projects to really think about what they wanted to say and make.

They created space to contemplate.

We make time for our family, we make time to get lost in the scroll of our phones, we make time to exercise, and have a meal with friends, but do we make time to contemplate?

Do we make time to really think about our lives? What we love? What we like? What interests us or compels us to create? Do we make time to wonder and dream without disruption?

We enter rooms and apps that tug on our insecurities, asking us to be reactive instead of intentional.

Audre Lorde famously wrote about living a life that is deliberate.

To be deliberate is to be powerful.

It demands stillness and patience. It is a rebellion against the culture of scarcity and toxic competition.

It takes us off the assembly line and plants us in an ecosystem that allows creativity, love, and the richness of our human experience.

you are invited

you are invited
to
be .
to
breathe
to break
free and away
even if only for a
minute
a single breath
the invitation has arrived
and your name
looks beautiful on it

Pause gifts us the space to be intentional and kind to ourselves as we pursue our goals. In pause we can ask ourselves if our difficulties are hurdles for us to leap over or roadblocks signaling us to move in a different direction. When our determination creates tunnel vision, there is no room for feeling or flexibility. It is important to get to where we want to go. It is equally important to be proud of who we are along the way.

Invite yourself to pause. Connect to your why. Connect to yourself. Our feelings create our flow.

We are very hard on each other.

The online world has given us so much access to each other's daily lives. Knowing someone more deeply can spark greater empathy, it can also spark greater judgment.

I often wonder if we are so critical of each other because the online windows we see each other through appear with a comment section underneath.

Whether you use that space or not, there is something about it being there that implies that everything we see needs our opinion. We have gotten very stuck in who is right, who is wrong, what is good, and what is bad.

When we are caught in judgment, we think we are in charge of what people do and don't deserve. "You don't deserve to feel sad, you have too much." "You don't deserve forgiveness, you've done too much." "You don't deserve happiness, you didn't do enough to earn it."

Being this judgmental covers us in muddy, unconstructive energy that is exhausting. Staying in it too long has the power to swallow you and distract you from your path.

Shame and judgment have never helped any situation. They don't lead to friendship, neighborliness, reconciliation, or anything else that improves our communities.

We ease the tension of our world when we release our grip on judgment and instead deliberately move toward empathy and wonder for those who are different from us.

someone who loves me

someone who loves me
gave me very sound
advice

feel the heat
the anger, the jealousy

get good and mad and green

then turn it into something

not hate, not judgment

turn it into wonder

wonder about them and wonder

about yourself

let the fire

turn into

light

We run into a lot of roadblocks on the way to I'm sorry. It can be difficult to acknowledge that we don't always get it right.

Sometimes it is the shame we feel when we make a mistake—we think ownership of the "bad thing" affirms that we are a "bad person." Sometimes we are still angry at the person we are in conflict with and don't feel they deserve our accountability. There are also many of us who didn't grow up around people who apologized, the healing power of the act was not modeled for us.

Whenever I make an error in judgment, say the wrong thing, hurt someone's feelings, make a mistake, or do any of the other zillion things that require an apology, I let these words guide my next step (even if I still feel a little hot or embarrassed by what happened):

I want to apologize. Not just for me. Not just for you. For us.

The words I'm sorry connect and reconnect us in moments of fracture. We apologize so we can all move forward, feeling seen and more deeply understood.

This is what healing looks like in community.

We have to want our healing and the healing of those we are in conflict with more than we want to be right or justified.

Self-righteousness alienates us. Humility bonds us.

If an apology is the only thing keeping you out in the cold, say I'm sorry, go back in the house, into the arms of your people.

WHEN WE OWN OUR ERRORS,
WHEN WE OFFER APOLOGY, WE
CONTRIBUTE TO COLLECTIVE
ONENESS. WE WANT OTHERS TO
FEEL SEEN AND OKAY BECAUSE
WE RECOGNIZE THAT THEIR
OKAY-NESS HOLDS HANDS WITH
OUR OKAY-NESS. DON'T LET YOUR
SILENCE GIVE WAY TO DISTANCE,
WHERE AN APOLOGY CAN CREATE
CONNECTION.

humility

there are two words
that more often than not
open

doors, arms, hearts, and new chapters:

I'm sorry

a gratitude prayer

your people are your stars

raise your gaze
hold the night's sky
between your eyelashes

connect the lights of your life
see the way the constellation
of people, your people, the people
who believe in you

illuminates everything

As someone who has been the believer and the believed in, I can say believing in someone is an incredible act of generosity—which happens to cost you nothing.

I can't think of anywhere worth getting to that we get to alone.

Everywhere I have gotten in my life is because someone believed in me. People who shone light on me when I was stumbling around in the dark. A teacher who thought I would do something special with my life. A boss who thought I belonged on a shelf in a bookstore instead of behind a desk in an office building. A friend who believed the notes I wrote myself in my notebook were more than just scribbles.

We live in gratitude when we acknowledge our support system.

We live in abundance when we are part of someone else's support system.

Whether it is telling someone that you love something they made or letting them know you are proud of them for doing something brave, we need these generous gestures from each other. They make moving forward less scary and remind us that we are not alone.

In a world that feels so lonely, why wouldn't we do that for each other?

I know we are all busy, but if you can, go out of your way for someone; you never know if it will change the direction of their life.

president of your fan club

I am a fan of changing your mind
of learning something new and allowing it
to change you

I am a fan of quitting what causes you harm
of saying

I used to do that
but now I don't do that anymore

I am a fan of transformation
being the deepest thing
that has ever happened to you

And also,
something that
merely is what it is:

for a long time, you were one way
and now you're this way

I am a fan of liberating yourself from
the cords that keep you too closely
connected to your
pain

of apologizing when
something didn't feel right

I'm sorry is
a shorthand for I see you
I know you're hurting,
and I take responsibility for myself

if you ask me, I'm sorry
is the blessing of all blessings

to be given and gotten
often and with a wide-open heart

I am a fan of freedom
of a life that feels
warm and lively

one that relates to the elements
sinking your feet in the earth
filling your body with fresh air

cooling your face and neck with clear blue water
covering yourself with the light of the sun's shine

we have all done some stuff
and been through some things

I am a fan of knowing that
of putting all of us in the same boat
a boat where we can take off
the armor of our saintliness

and sit in mercy and grace

I am a fan of one day at a time
and of trying
always trying
of falling and getting up

and of clichés because
they're true and half the time
they're helping us to be better people

I'm a fan of you

who you've been and
who you're becoming

the parts of your long walk
that got a little grim

the parts that were lovely
and smelled like lavender

I'm a fan

Are you happy for others?

The idea that we be happy for others seems obvious and maybe even easy, but in this era of compulsive comparison, a lot of us struggle to offer this simple blessing.

To embody true joy in a way that wishes joy for others is a deeply spiritual practice. It requires an almost religious devotion, a moment-to-moment choosing and re-choosing of the kind of person you want to be. It is an active decision to alchemize emotions like jealousy into something helpful.

One way we can do this is by hanging out in the feelings. Staying in them as an observer. Releasing thoughts about the other person and asking yourself what may be underneath your reaction.

I once heard someone say that jealousy can be useful as long as you don't turn it into harm.

Jealousy is a powerful emotion with a lot of information. If we allow it to filter through our inner wisdom, it can act as a signal directing us towards what we want. It is only destructive if you allow it to manifest in the world unprocessed.

Jealousy doesn't have to say, "I want that. You shouldn't have it."

We can turn it into, "I want that. I'm grateful for what I see in your journey because it is helping me clarify my goals."

We react. It is human. Our first thought is not often in our control but our next thought is usually our choice.

To live with joy and want joy for others is to live with the best possible energy. It is an energy that attracts and spreads goodness, that keeps you motivated and inspires others. It is the definition of good vibes. It is a sustainable magic that can shift almost any circumstance.

I recently asked Cheryl Strayed how she defined vulnerability.

She said,

"Vulnerability is being honest about who you are and what you are going through."

Words like vulnerability and authenticity are so widely used, it is hard to understand exactly what they are or how to practice them.

It is difficult to be honest about who we are. There are parts of ourselves we don't love, can't look at, and hope no one notices as we sweep them under the rug. We have pasts that haunt us, shame that follows us around like a shadow at high noon. Everything we can't forgive or give grace pushes us into a daze of dishonesty, often leaving us feeling estranged and lonely.

We can't connect because we can't be vulnerable--we can't be honest with those we love about who we are and what we are going through. We can't see our needs because we are afraid to view ourselves with honest eyes.

I was this way for a long time. My connections were wide but not deep. I wanted to be the person who was always okay. The person who was never bothered or hurt. If I flooded those around me with helpful, giving energy, then I wouldn't have to ask myself what I had gone through or was going through that needed help and healing.

I think a large part of this is because I didn't have a safe or brave space to be vulnerable. I wasn't surrounded by people I felt could love me as I was. I am not even sure I felt I could love me the way I was.

Cheryl's definition offered so much clarity to my traveled road. I never knew how to be vulnerable. I didn't wake up one morning and think, I want to be more vulnerable. I really didn't understand that word.

I did, however, wake up one morning and say I'm ready to look at my life with the most honest possible eyes. I'd read a book of poems by Hafiz that led me on a yearlong-journey of devouring books in the spirituality and self-help aisles.

There was something in me that was tired of the shallow end, I wanted to learn to swim. I sought out relationships that could hold my honesty and help me unearth the parts of myself and my story I'd buried. I met new people, I fell into a closer, deeper, more intimate bond with old friends, I worked to mend or at least minimize my wounds. A few years later I wrote *Heart Talk,* my first book.

It is easy to float through the world. But good God, if you can learn to swim, I do recommend it.

it be this way sometimes

I expected more
they couldn't give more
I asked everyone what to do with how
much this hurt me
finally, grace replied and said
forgive
move on
they did the best they could
if they could have done better
they would have

YOU ARE ALLOWED TO BE A BALL
OF CONTRADICTIONS. EVERYTHING
YOU ARE AND EVERYTHING YOU
LIKE DOES NOT HAVE TO MAKE
SENSE IN RELATION TO EACH
OTHER. LIFE IS LESS ABOUT
BEING RIGHT, CORRECT, AND
VALIDATED AND MORE ABOUT
BEING FREE, JOYFUL, AND
CURIOUS. IN A WORLD THAT ASKS
YOU TO SEE IT IN BLACK AND
WHITE—DO YOURSELF THE DIVINE
FAVOR OF EXPERIENCING IT IN
COLOR.

One of my girlfriends said the best advice she's ever received is that other people's opinions of her are none of her business.

Another friend told me she is happy when people like her, but she doesn't need people to like her in order to be happy.

These are powerful and worthy rebellions.

We must let go of worrying about and controlling other people's opinions of us. We have a great responsibility to ourselves to pursue freedom and joy. It is very hard to get there when the voice of our inner-GPS is the validations or judgments of others.

There is great peace to be found in allowing people's feelings to belong to them. That does not mean we shut ourselves off from others, it just means we don't allow pleasing others to give direction to our lives.

I have been through many conflicts. I have had to quit jobs, fire people, break up with people, get broken up with, fall out with friends, sever ties with family members. I'm sure there are a lot of people who have left a confrontation or situation with me feeling disappointed or upset because they did not get their way.

I used to feel the need for everyone I interacted with to like me, even during and after conflict. It was hard for me to stand up for myself because I feared their negative reaction to my needed boundaries. I would betray my own integrity and self-kindness in the hope they would think I was a good or nice person. This gave others a lot of power over me.

Why was someone other than me deciding if I was a good or nice person?

I decide the quality of my character. I know who I am, and in knowing who I am, I can let go of other people's opinions of who I am.

You liberate yourself when you allow others to have their side of the story.

I found a children's book called *Ping* by Ani Castillo in my daughter's room. The first page says, "My friend, in this life . . . we can only Ping. The Pong belongs to the other."

May you live boldly in your ping.

PART THREE

notes on heartbreak

IT IS A PROFOUND ACT OF LOVE
TO CHOOSE WHO YOU ARE GOING
TO BE INSTEAD OF LIVING IN
RESPONSE TO WHO HAS HURT YOU
AND WHAT HAS HAPPENED TO
YOU. TO MAKE YOUR HEART YOUR
DIVINE RESPONSIBILITY. TO
CHALLENGE YOURSELF TO GET
YOUR HEART AS KIND AND
FIERCELY LOVING AS POSSIBLE.
IT IS A PROFOUND ACT OF
COURAGE TO THEN SHARE THAT
HEART WITH THE WORLD.

bell hooks defined love as a combination of care, commitment, knowledge, responsibility, respect, and trust.

Love feels like a giant, spectacular, abstract force most of the time.

The spiritual practice of love asks us to live in awe of its hugeness.

The practical practice of love, one that lives in and builds more meaningful community with our friends, romantic partners, and family members, asks us to create a healthy and nourishing definition. It asks us to know what love is and how it behaves, so that we may know when to protect it, when to nourish it, when to request it, and when to let go of something masquerading as it.

cleo wade

My mom recently emailed me a photograph of a school project from first grade. We were asked to write a valentine to our parents naming the ways we show them love. Mine read:

I show my love for you by being quiet when you are on the phone, I show my love for you by going to bed on time, I show my love for you by washing the dishes.

I was seven years old and had already concluded that showing love meant being cooperative and making someone else's life easier. I am grateful I was raised to be deeply considerate of others (especially my mom, who was a single mother struggling to make ends meet), but I often wonder at what point does consideration turn into the type of accommodation that erases us in relationships.

I have watched the patterns from my childhood lead me to live in the shadows of those I love as an adult. I spent a lot of time thinking my value was rooted in how valuable I made other people feel.

In one relationship, my valentine would have read:

I show my love for you by focusing on your dreams instead of my own. I show my love for you by prioritizing your health and healing instead of my own. I show my love for you by centering your needs instead of my own.

What is a pattern? Something that repeats over and over again. Our patterns can be our history without becoming our destiny. We don't have to repeat what we know.

We have the power to course-correct. It is unnecessary and unwise to allow our past to dictate the direction of our future.

Letting go of old habits and investing in new ones can often feel like we are turning a big boat in a rough sea. Slow and uncomfortable.

But isn't a better, truer love worth it?

P.S. I write valentines to myself now. The first one said,

I show my love for you by living beyond the love you learned in search of the love you deserve.

I hear someone knocking

what will become of her?
will she keep finding you?

a you
that is someone else
but still
you

will she keep choosing a love
that only loves itself

or

will she change

will she become
someone new
find
someone new
and finally
arrive
at the door of
a love
that loves back

cleo wade

I returned the cape

he keeps calling me superwoman
he means it as a compliment
but
superwoman is not
a real person

when you are superhuman, you don't get to be human

People, regardless of how high functioning they are, need to be able to be people. Untidy. Overwhelmed. Falling apart. Tired. In tears. In need.

When we call someone a superhero, we are usually treating them like one. Like someone whose sole purpose in the story is to save the day or die trying. We may think it is high praise, but we are either consciously or subconsciously asking them to deal with or handle more than a human being should have to.

There is a scene in the movie *The Philadelphia Story* where Katharine Hepburn's character's fiancé is telling her all of the reasons he admires her. He likens her to a queen and a beautiful statue. He tells her he worships her. She looks away and says, "I don't want to be worshipped. I want to be loved." People do not need to be wor-

shipped or admired for what they are able to endure with a smile.

People need to be people.

People need to be loved.

heart, mind, body

we cannot only build empires
we must build homes—places our eyes can close and find
    warmth by the fire

our hearts cannot survive in skyscrapers
our hearts want to leave their shoes at the door of a nearby
    forest and follow the trail
our hearts want to feel the hum of the hummingbird

and the busy mind
it needs sun and sky
it begs to hear the nearby stream wash over its endless
    thoughts

of course, I cannot forget the body
it told me to tell you
it would like to dance and run free
also, it kindly requested a quiet squeeze and an "I love you"
as soon as you get a chance

A RELATIONSHIP MAY FEEL LIKE
WORK BUT LOVING SOMEONE
SHOULD NEVER FEEL LIKE A JOB.

It is important to give and do for others. It is also important to notice if your partner's or friend's respect, praise, and love are contingent on whether you are giving and doing for them.

Your relationship cannot rely on your labor. Your person cannot be your job.

Yes, there is work to be done.

We work on our issues, our patterns, our healing. We work on the shared stuff.

But it is not sustainable to function for another person or live with their experience at the center of your existence. When we try to do this (and I have tried), we end up exhausted, resentful, and disconnected from ourselves.

cleo wade

Our relationships are powerful when they are fueling stations, the places we fill up, not the places we are drained.

We don't work for those we love, we work with them. A loving relationship is a collaboration. We contribute to a shared and sacred experience.

Are things falling apart or falling away? Life consistently asks us to shed. We shed relationships, we shed jobs and lifestyles, we shed interests, ideas, and judgments. I used to think rock bottom was the worst place we could end up. It is actually the place most of us rediscovered and repaired our foundation so we could rebuild our lives with love and intention.

The moments I have felt the most alone were also the moments I could hear myself the loudest. I thought my life was falling apart but, really, the noise that led me awry had fallen away. In the moments I felt the most heartbroken, lying on the couch alone and in tears, I was gifted self-intimacy. The voice of the person I'd been with had become louder than my own. When I could hear myself clearly, I was given a chance to get to know myself again. I was able to dream again and make new decisions for myself.

Release is not only a relief, it is often a catalyst. The trees release their leaves and flowers. They lay bare all winter long—but they are not dead, they are preparing for newness. We have these periods too; when we have moments of transition and feel like we don't have a friend in the world, or move through divorce and incredible grief. Big parts of life are falling away, but you remain. You have the power to alchemize your pain point into a starting point, when you're ready, when the time is right.

turning the page

after it has all been
said and done

and

what is done
cannot be
undone

I let go (of you)
because you don't
belong to me
& hold on (to myself)
because I do

I sit alone, I rest, I give, I feel
and I get ready for tomorrow

the end of our story is not the end of my story

I am often asked about how to get through heartbreak.

Here are a couple of ideas I am in favor of holding on to:

1. You are already getting through it.

2. The ending of a relationship with someone else is usually followed by the beginning of a new relationship with yourself. One you may not have expected but probably needed.

Heartbreak is a place of deep feeling. When we swim beyond the pain, sadness, loss, and fear, we find our power to learn, change, and grow.

I've had my heart broken.

I have learned that if we own our heartbreak and don't let it take ownership of us (I know this is hard to imagine if you are in the thick of it), it can be the catalyst that transforms the most important relationship in your life, the one with yourself.

I have never met anyone who has not gained deeper knowledge of themselves during the process of heartbreak.

Finding this wisdom is how we begin to heal.

what to do when your heart breaks

enter through the wound
lie down on the floor
of your determined heart

breathe

let it show you how
it beats beyond defeat
let it show you how
endings become beginnings

I asked my friend's very wise mother about divorce. She told me the thing about happiness is you don't think during it. You're too busy enjoying it. When we are in a state of joy we are almost always fully in the present moment, living beyond our thoughts, fears, and anxieties. She said, pain causes us to question our life. We ask, *Why me? Why this? How could this happen? What is making me feel this way?*

Our ability to question and interrogate our lives is a large part of how we intentionally choose our path. We often hear people tell us that we need pain, without it we wouldn't know the greatness of joy. Perhaps without it, we wouldn't know what direction brings us closer to finding and feeling joy.

When you are heartbroken, all you do is ask yourself questions:

What didn't I see? How could things have been different?

When a relationship has run its course and you are faced with grief and sadness as you tell someone you love that it's over, all you do in the days that lead up to that moment is ask yourself questions:

Why do I feel different? Why isn't this enough? What more could I ask for?

I hate that our hearts break. But in these pieces, in the damage, the pain, the ache, the tears we find the questions.

When forever doesn't last forever, we get to ask ourselves why.

The why. The questions. They lead us somewhere. Somewhere new and sometimes needed.

When you are emotionally committed to someone who won't commit to you, it is as if you are going through a breakup every other day.

We try and we try to get them to see the light and if they don't, we create stories that give us reason to stay: They love me but they have some family stuff to work through. They love me but they need to focus on their career. They love me but they are happier living in Europe right now. (One time I literally thought I could make it work with a guy who actively put an ocean between us.)

When our commitment is continually unmet, we end up feeling sad and let down more often than happy and fulfilled.

A love worthy of your time is one that feels like equal devotion. When someone wants to turn their love for you into a real relationship, they commit to being together in a way that feels good for both of you. You won't feel like you are getting the short end of the stick. You won't need excuses or justifications. Your love will be in motion toward union and communication. For love to work in a relationship, we have to choose pathways that lead us towards each other.

Commitment moves us closer and closer to closeness.

narcissa

I want you to fall in love with me
not the parts of me you need

I don't want to be strong because your love for me requires
my strength

I don't want to be understanding because your love for me
    requires
that I understand the ways you hurt me

I don't want a love that asks me
to sit
as you sing in the spotlight

I want a love that knows

I have a song too

know this

love
will ask you
to make many compromises
but it will never
ask you
to compromise
yourself

It can be scary to draw boundaries, communicate our needs plainly, or put our feelings on the map. Sometimes this is because we feel the other person can't handle it or will abandon us if we are not easy and accommodating. Other times we fear that if our needs don't match what they are willing to give, the relationship will end.

Relationships are the space we create from love. They cannot be lawless or defined by the strongest personality in the dynamic.

They also cannot reside in gray areas for prolonged periods of time. Periods of indecision and noncommitment can be helpful as we get to know someone, but over time, especially when this desire is not mutual, they become maddening and hurtful.

We respect each other by building sanctuaries for our connections. These safe spaces are only safe when everyone involved is honest, fully expressed, and cared for.

If your relationship is not in flow, start with how you feel and align on what you both want and are capable of. When two people have a shared vision, it is easier to co-create boundaries and practices that can support it.

your tides

I swam in your tides
for too long
the waters were a deep, and dark,
and at times a very beautiful blue color

they were also temperamental and tiresome

I thought
maybe I'm just not
trying hard enough
maybe
I need to learn
to swim better

time passed me by
and in the midst of my treading
I wondered:

what would happen if I stopped
fighting this current?

I put my head back

I let myself float to warmer water

your waves began to fade
and feel unfamiliar

and slowly, slowly, slowly,
I found
the safety of my own shore

it's called saving yourself

When in the process of trying to let go of a relationship, one of the most important questions we can ask ourselves is:

What do I want more than this person?

Do I want stability more than this person? Do I want a family more than this person? Do I want easeful joy more than this person? Do I want freedom more than this person?

When I was twenty I "dated" someone who never took me on a date. He just invited me to hang out at his apartment all the time. I *cringe* now thinking about all of the ways I romanticized our dynamic.

One night, I was at a hole-in-the-wall jazz bar in the East Village with my girlfriends and was having the time of my life. We danced, drank whiskey, laughed, and talked until we lost our voices.

I remember thinking to myself, this is it. This is what I want my life to feel like. In that moment, even though I loved him, the relationship became impossible. I had to let go of the dream that we would be together.

I wanted the life I wanted more than I wanted this person.

My feelings for him didn't disappear, I was sad. It was hard to walk away (and took many attempts), but when I asked myself what I had to compromise in order to make the "relationship" work, the answer was . . . me.

I had to compromise myself and the life I wanted.

Our lives are bigger than one relationship.

We must give ourselves permission to have the lives we want. We must give ourselves permission to let go of one dream and dream up something or someone new. Doing this helps us move on when the one we want does not fit into the life we want.

Ten years ago, someone gifted me a session with an astrologer in San Francisco who introduced me to the idea of a soul contract.

She said all our connections have a soul contract. Our souls are meant to be with other souls in a specific way for a specific amount of time. And when a relationship is experiencing constant friction, it can be a sign that the contract is outdated and we need to either create a new one with new terms or part ways.

She felt all our relationships were written in the stars.

I found beauty and practicality in this.

We often need new soul contracts with friends when big life changes happen—moving, loss of a parent, new job, partnering, or having kids.

As we grow older in our family of origin, we often need new soul contracts with our elders that acknowledge our independence and evolving identity.

Recently, I spent time with a friend who was grappling with her divorce from a man who cheated on her. We discussed the idea that their soul contract as romantic partners had been violated and couldn't be renewed so they had to draw up a new one as co-parents.

Soul contracts are not written formal agreements. They are more of an acknowledgment of what we need and how we want to be treated in our relationships. They are also an acknowledgment that we are not meant to be with everyone we love forever. Our relationships will shift and change and end. Some soul contracts last until we are ninety-nine and some expire sooner than the milk in our refrigerator. Trust the stars.

Betrayal throws us out of our bodies. We go into shock, are overwhelmed with anger, scramble to fix the situation, or punish the other person. We rarely give ourselves time to feel. Whether it is a betrayal of trust from our romantic partner, friend, family member, or colleague, we can only truly move forward when we have given ourselves space to sit with our emotions.

When I was betrayed, I felt lost. And sometimes the best and only thing to do when you feel lost is pull over and recalibrate. Feel what you feel, reflect on the many roads that got you to where you are, and give yourself time before moving forward.

Because the energy around betrayal is often frenzied and dramatic, it causes us to rush into decision making. We want to hurry up and fix it or control it. This is not a helpful headspace when making a major decision. We need calm. We need self-connectedness.

We need time to heal. Our open wounds cannot be the place from

which we decide what to do next.

What I know about betrayal is that recovery is possible. Whether

it is with or without the person who hurt you. We can comfort

ourselves. We can find steadiness in dizzying territory. We can seek

council and support. We can step away from the person who hurt

us or lean into the shared labor of forgiveness and redemption.

Whatever you decide, the key is to avoid decision making when

you are feeling your worst.

YOUR SOCIAL CIRCLES ARE NOT
ALWAYS YOUR HEALING CIRCLES.

Everyone in your life does not belong *everywhere* in your life.

When we are moving through grief, tragedy, or trauma, it is important to recognize that our social circles are not necessarily our healing circles.

Healing requires safety.

We cannot heal if we don't feel safe.

This is a sad truth, but even the people we love and trust the most don't always know how to make us feel safe when we are hurting.

Periods of pain require different levels of emotional availability from everyone involved.

When we are in pain, we often need a very specific energy from others in order to feel held and soothed.

cleo wade

We may need new and unexpected friends or resources and find that friends we see often, though treasured, are not the support we need.

That is okay.

When you are at your most fragile, give yourself permission to surround yourself with the people who can be what you need.

The people who can be with your bubble-wrapped heart and handle it with care.

help that is helpful

if you fall into the mud
do not befriend its residents
reach out your hand
find help from someone
living on the lotus

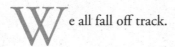

We all fall off track.

We put in a ton of work to go ten feet forward and fall twenty feet back.

When this happens, we must lean on the people who want for us the goodness we want for ourselves.

If you are in a dark or negative place, you will always find people living in that energy.

These are not your helping hands.

If we are hanging on the edge, someone who is also hanging on the edge cannot help us up; we need someone who is on top of the ledge to pull us up.

When we struggle, we often look for people going through the same thing. Connecting through shared experiences can be comforting and bonding.

But we have to make sure that those people do not want us to stay where we are if it is an unhealthy place.

We need people who want us to get better and feel better. We need people who can help us up when we fall.

No one is entitled to hurt you or cause you pain. No one.

We often think there is something wrong with us when we need to put people on pause or sever ties because they are causing us pain or blocking our pathway to healing. Distance is not always avoidance. Distance is sometimes the boundary we need in order to heal from the hurt caused by others, and avoid reinjury.

I know how sad it feels when the people we love or care for don't know how to treat us. They take advantage of our kindness or generosity. They say harmful things to bring us down or manipulate us. Whether it stems from their own trauma or lack of tools, some people only meet you with toxicity no matter how much love you give.

When we are in community with a person—whether a friend, family member (even a parent), or romantic partner—who is unable to uplift us, we are always allowed to take a step away. You are always allowed to protect your peace or keep yourself safe.

WHEN YOU LOVE SOMEONE, MADE
MEMORIES WITH THEM, GREW
WITH AND BECAUSE OF THEM,
THE SPIRIT OF THAT BOND IS
ALWAYS ALIVE SOMEWHERE
WITHIN YOU. THE PEOPLE WE
LOVE ARE NOT ALWAYS MEANT TO
STAY WITH US FOREVER BUT
MAYBE THERE IS GRATITUDE TO
BE FOUND IN GOODBYE. AND
MAYBE AS YOU MOVE ON, IT IS
POSSIBLE TO MOVE FURTHER
FROM PAIN AND CLOSER TO
APPRECIATION.

I am not sure we can unlove people. Love feels like a line within. Once crossed, those who get in seem to stay in.

I love friends I don't talk to. I love exes I'm glad I didn't end up with. I still love my seventh-grade teacher Ms. Ory, who I haven't seen or spoken to in over twenty years.

When we part ways with people, especially in friendship breakups, we feel hurt and try very hard to disconnect the love because we think doing that will ease the pain of separation.

As someone who has gone through a few friendship breakups, my only advice is:

Don't mess with the love.

cleo wade

You might need to put distance there. Or distance might put itself there. You might move to a different city, move in with a partner, or move into a different phase of life.

We change and grow away from even the people we love the most.

I do think, even if the relationship isn't there, leave the love.

If the love spoiled into something else over time, remember when it was good, let that memory remain, release the rest.

I have had friendships come back after a decade of dormancy. I have some that are still lost in the woods. Others that have come back in different forms; we see each other occasionally, have play-dates with our kids. The day-to-day-ness is gone, but the love and admiration are still felt.

You never know who will come back around. The ultimate gift in life is a familiar face. Someone who knows you deeply. Someone who has loved you wholly.

And if life does not bring you back together at least, as the old saying goes, there is no love lost between you.

SOMETIMES THE PEOPLE YOU LOVE
NEED SPACE TO BREATHE,
STUMBLE, LEARN, GROW, AND DO
BETTER TOMORROW THAN THEY
COULD TODAY.

A few years ago, on a late-night walk in my neighborhood in New York, I was talking to a friend about what happens when we love someone who doesn't love us back.

I had been stuck in a cycle of giving my all to someone who gave me their crumbs.

I was feeling really sorry for myself when my friend asked me,

What do you believe?

Do you believe that this is the only person you are meant to be with for your entire life? Of all the people you have met? Of all the people you will ever meet?

I'd never considered that my beliefs had been guiding my feelings and behavior.

When I got home that night I continued to question my beliefs.

Do I believe that I show up for love but love doesn't have to show up for me? Do I believe that feeling bad is a part of love? Do I believe that someone other than myself should be in charge of my happiness?

When I dissected my beliefs, I found I wasn't committed to this person, I was committed to a belief system that reflected the deeper struggles I had with feeling worthy of kind, consistent, and nourishing love.

Much of our low self-esteem comes from our unhealed experiences. Through reflection and with support from my friends and therapist, I began journeying through my past so I could heal my open wounds and build self-worth.

Loving myself more thoroughly made me believe I was deserving

of more thorough love from others.

Our beliefs are powerful, they drive the direction of our lives, they

tell us what feels right and what feels wrong, what we are worthy

of, and who we can trust.

how it goes

it's been
raining & raining & raining
& raining

it rained so much
it felt like it would rain forever

then one day

at 5:30 p.m.

abruptly, with no notice at all

the sky was dry, clear, hot pink, and orange

there was even a little purple woven in

that's what it's like isn't it?
your heart is broken
and every day is sad
until
one day all at once
with no notice

you find beauty again

when it's time, it's time

it's time to open up again.

I know your heart broke
and it took more time
than you ever imagined
to sew patches over your cracks

it looks different
it feels different
it is different

still
it's time to open again

even after all you've been through

even if you're scared
even if you're scarred

it's time to open up again

cleo wade

THE DIVINE INVESTIGATION INTO
YOUR OWN HEART IS THE
EDUCATION OF YOUR LIFETIME.

Our behavior ripples through our community. How daunting. And also, how divine.

We have no idea how many people our energy touches in a day. We have no idea how many people notice how we love ourselves and those around us.

Do we live with the awareness that someone is learning how to love based on our behavior?

James Baldwin wrote, "Children have never been very good at listening to their elders, but they have never failed to imitate them."

I've been the kid who absorbed everything, and now I have kids who absorb everything.

It took me many years to shed the ideas about love that were shown to me in my childhood. I was chasing the love I saw growing up. One that was often unkind and required frequent forgiveness from women. I am not even sure it was love. It was more like something that demanded you call it love.

When I had kids, I was grateful for the time I'd spent practicing how to love others well. I didn't want my family of origin or a movie telling me what love was and how it behaved. I wanted to invent it for myself, based on my own research and inquiries in the heart.

I didn't want my life to be an imitation.

I wanted it to be my own.

I wanted my behavior to be something I was proud made a ripple.

generous

love is a sharing thing
it is not
a reward for your efforts
you sit at the table
you pass the potatoes
serve your beloved the gravy
they put
some peas on your plate
you take more, they take less
you take less, they take more
each of us deserving of our serving
love is a Sunday dinner
there is enough to go around

PART FOUR

& then we let go

new beginnings

we live
in a world
of
sunrises

if the earth is given a chance to start over every single day,
    aren't you?

S tarting over is a part of our nature.

We end one breath and take in another each second. We witness death and birth. We watch trees turn bare and bloom again in spring.

Life is a big beginning and a big ending, with lots of little beginnings and endings in between.

We must let relationships run their course without fear and guilt.

We must love our bodies through change without shame and disappointment.

We must welcome new phases of life without defiance.

Too many of our endings are more painful than they need to be because we are not allowing them to turn into new beginnings.

ROCK BOTTOM IS A BOTTOM.
A PLACE WHERE WE ARE GIVEN
THE OPPORTUNITY TO ENCOUNTER
AND STRENGTHEN OUR
FOUNDATION. WE CAN LAND
THERE AND WE CAN BUILD
FROM THERE.

how to do the thing you are afraid to do

grab fear's hand

grab hope's hand

start walking

I have stopped using the word fearless lately.

I used to think we could outgrow or work ourselves away from fear. I am not sure about that now. I think fear is always present. It is a part of our aliveness, our personhood. Trying to ignore it or outsmart it tends to misplace it and sometimes even gives it the power to dictate the direction of our lives.

When I work with and learn to accept the presence of big feelings like fear, impostor syndrome, and self-doubt, I can say okay, you are here, where do you belong? Doing this returns my power to me. It takes these feelings out of the driver's seat, and even if I can't throw them out of the window, I can put them in the backseat or the trunk (if I'm lucky).

Everything we feel is useful information, our great task is to decide

what to do with it and how to use it to move us towards what we

want and deserve.

I never tell my daughters not to cry.

We are told not to cry our whole lives. At home. At school. At work.

I once told my therapist I wasn't good at crying.

I hid my tears for so long, they began hiding from me.

Nikki Giovanni wrote:

"we are strong enough to stand tall tearlessly, we are brave enough to bend to cry, and we are sad enough to know that we must laugh again."

Maybe we find our tears through our bravery. Bravery is usually something we inch toward (unless something gigantic gives us a big push—which is sometimes amazing and other times the worst).

If you are inching, it helps to surround yourself with tenderness. I am positive I found my tears because I found tender people to hold my tears safely when I was finally ready to let them go.

I never tell my daughters not to cry. I hold them and tell them to let it out. Release.

The world may ask them to be strong all the time, but their mother will not. I'd rather they be courageous. I'd rather they be free.

a release

the tears
they shed and shed

it is a gift
it is a gift to have a body
that will let go of
what I can no longer hold

I let the water wash away the stories that
have turned into cargo ships carrying
too much of my past to bear

I let the water tell me
what belongs on the shore
and what belongs to the sea

each wave
takes what it takes

a release

each wave
takes what it takes

a release

a little water
it is a gift
it is my gift

the thing about aliveness

wherever you are
sitting, standing, running, chasing, smiling, screaming,
   crying
still or in motion
life is happening
you are alive

cleo wade

EVERYONE WANTS WHAT THEY
WANT REGARDLESS OF WHAT YOU
CAN GIVE. IF YOU WANT FREEDOM
AND PERSONAL PEACE, YOU HAVE
TO LEARN TO BE OKAY WITH
LETTING PEOPLE DOWN AND
LETTING PEOPLE GO.

When we wear masks for too long, we struggle to locate ourselves beneath them.

A few years ago, I ended a consuming relationship and was buried beneath the mask of trying to be the perfect partner. I'd been giving and fixing and trying to hold every piece together just right for years.

Even after we broke up, I felt stuck in a pattern of being really stiff and uptight. I needed to loosen up. I got on a plane and went to Mardi Gras in New Orleans for the weekend. I dressed in outrageous costumes, I danced in the street, I ate po'boys and drank beer on the curb, I twirled, I sang. I let go of caring what anyone thought and I got weird. A weekend of being free and goofy is what got me back to myself. The happiness I felt being my weird self is what helped get me through the breakup. It helped me see that I wanted a relationship where I could be liberated from the need to wear a mask.

If you're wearing a mask right now, and it's been on so long you're not sure who you are without it, here is the invitation to remove it. Get honest. Get weird. Claiming and enjoying our wild uniqueness melts away the things in life that tell us we have to be something other than what we are.

Quitting is not always failure.

It can sometimes be the only way to give ourselves the care we need to make room for something new.

I think we should want a lot out of life. Lots of goals. Lots of dreams. Lots of love.

There is much to be gained from having discipline and seeing things through to completion.

We must also trust the signs around us that let us know completion is near. Completion cannot be prescribed by social norms, the opinions of others, or what we hoped it would look like.

I would still have my old day job if I had listened to my parents the day I decided to quit. I have many friends who would never have blossomed into their full potential as women without quitting relationships or marriages that didn't support their growth.

When we change, or the world around us changes (especially in the ways it has in the past few years), we have to let our goals change, we have to let our minds change, we have to let our hearts change.

Quitting is often a part of letting go.

Forgiveness is not a decision, it is a devotional practice.

We weave forgiveness into our lives like a prayer.

Every morning and every evening, I ask for and extend forgiveness.

May I forgive myself. May I forgive those who hurt me. May I forgive those I needed more from and could not give to me because they didn't know how. May those I have hurt feel and live with forgiveness for me.

Opening and closing my days with these words helps console what is unsettled from my past.

We often try to substitute forgiving with forgetting. We try to forget what happened to us.

We try to forget people.

We try to forget what we have done in our past.

We try and try and try and try. Trying to forget is feverish labor that distracts us from our suffering without healing it. We lie awake in the middle of the night rushed with feelings of resentment, anger, and disappointment.

Unforgiveness is life with a storm beneath our skin.

When we try towards forgiveness each day, especially self-forgiveness, we begin to clear the clouds.

this or that

here,
take the mask

I would like you to see me

I would like to see myself

I would like to see the world

the longer it's on, the more you realize, you can either have
a mask or a real life. There isn't a third option.

maybe the only thing

who you were
is who you are
is who you will be

every chapter is a part of the book

the best thing, and maybe the only thing, we can do with
    the blunders, the shame, the remorse, is wrap the whole
    thing in
love

ghosts & angels

I practice forgetting &
everything I try to forget
becomes a ghost

I practice forgiving &
everything I try to forgive
becomes an angel

this spirit befriends me
it does not follow me around
lurking in my darkness
it leads me someplace new
someplace that lives in my light

In my first month living in New York City as a teenager, my purse was stolen at a nightclub I snuck into.

A few weeks later, I was still upset about it and an older (and much wiser) woman I knew said, "If it is gone, give it away. If you give it away with your blessing, it was never taken from you. You don't have to live with the burden of being done to."

It was a lesson on how the energy we wrap around our experiences often dictates our ability to move on.

That evening, I thought about how I'd once found twenty dollars as I was walking on the street. I thought it was the best day ever. I didn't consider that if I found it, then someone else lost it.

I remember saying to myself, I'm letting go of this. I am letting go of not only the thing, but the entire situation.

That was the first time I realized we had the power to give away what is upsetting us.

I learned release.

I have had to release more monumental things than handbags over the years—people, jobs, friendships, relationships with family members. The lesson still applies.

So much of what we hold on to is our own energy. We hold anger because we feel we wasted our time. We hold disappointment because we feel our expectations weren't met. We hold guilt because we had to leave certain relationships in order to be happy.

We can release these energies. We can bless these experiences.

Gratitude is not just about selectively seeing and appreciating the

good in your life. It is about pulling the good from the difficult

and allowing it to inform and strengthen you.

everything that's happened

there are some very large letting goes to do:
people, places, honeyed and bitter phases of life
there are some even larger letting goes to do:
anger, tears, parts of yourself that leave with no return

have a past

everything that's happened cannot be held today

OUR PROBLEMS ARE OFTEN THE PART OF OUR PROCESS WE DIDN'T KNOW WE NEEDED.

S urrender is a big idea.

We may know where we want to go in life, but we surrender to the fact that we have no idea how we will get there.

We can try to control as many circumstances as possible, we can do things that make part of the journey more predictable, but, with almost everything in life, there is a part of the story that goes, "and if I hadn't met this person, I would have never . . ." or "everything changed when I saw . . ."

Allow yourself to not know. Envisioning what you want is deeply helpful. But trying to calculate the exact year, way it happens, or people it happens with is usually a sign our fear and ego have taken the wheel.

cleo wade

Some of the best advice anyone ever gave me was "don't put a face on it." I was talking to a friend about dating. She told me to hold the qualities I wanted, rather than the specific person. Don't envision being with Bob, envision being with a good listener. Envision being with a person who wants to be in a committed loving relationship.

What we want manifests in ways beyond our expectations. Trying to control every detail blocks our blessings and makes it difficult to see that what we want may be right in front of us or already within us.

When I was writing this book there was a power outage in my neighborhood, I lost almost half of the book due to a computer glitch. I crawled into bed and cried.

Two days later, I got up and went back to work. I thought about those words. Don't put a face on it.

I knew the kind of book I waned to write, but I didn't know how or on what day it was going to happen. In the days that followed, I had more flow and clarity than I'd had in weeks.

It turns out my process needed that "problem." It shifted me into the gear I needed to be able to cross the finish line.

When I surrendered, I could start again. And I could finish.

We don't know. Knowing this can be scary or a relief (if we let it).

The meant-to-be moments often follow the mishaps. Letting go of how we think it is supposed to be often makes room for the way it needs to be.

The how doesn't belong to us.

I met my current partner at a party celebrating my ex.

He bumped into me as he turned the corner from the stairs.

We now have two daughters.

Who'd have known?

Not me.

meant to

we grasp and grasp
but life is air
life is water
it is not meant to be tightly squeezed
we are meant to move as the breeze
coming and going
a rain that returns to the clouds
eventually

transformation

transformation involves
a lot of goodbyes

allow the grief

let yourself love the one(s) you had to leave
let yourself have fond memories
let yourself find peace in the world you turned upside
  down because you were brave enough to change

ACKNOWLEDGMENTS

This book was built on long walks, long distance phone calls, and long nights next to the fireplace with take-out containers, red wine, tears of relief, and delirious laughter. I smile as I write this. I am so damn grateful to those I get to love and do life with.

Thank you to my miraculous friends and family, especially Simon and our people. The Wades & Kinbergs make a killer combo if you ask me.

Thank you to Amy Sherald for your guidance and the vibrant life you gave this cover.

To Cait Hoyt and Shannon Welch, thank you for believing in this book. Your thoughtful feedback and gentle encouragement pushed me to challenge myself in new ways.

To the ancestors, the many writers who created pathways for writers like me to exist. Eternal gratitude.

Lastly, to you, my readers, you have made my dreams come true. Thank you for allowing me and to be a part of your life. It is the great gift of my life and I treasure it.